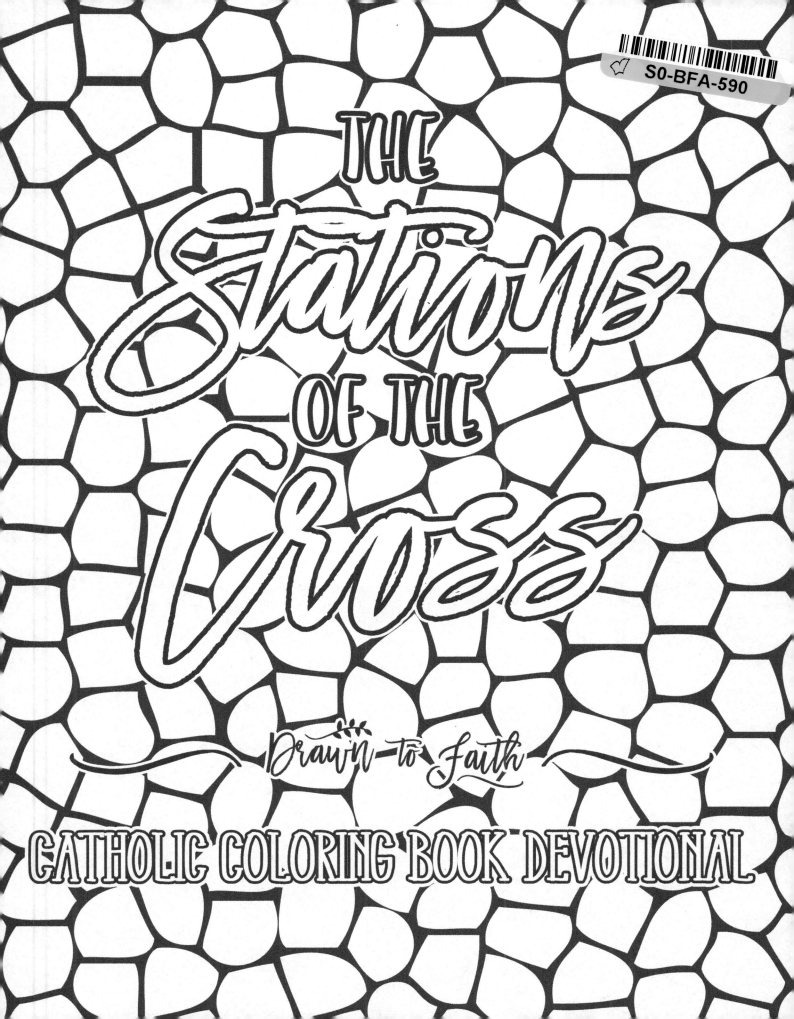

THE Stations OF THE Cross

Drawn to Faith

CATHOLIC COLORING BOOK DEVOTIONAL

Illustrated by Maryna

ISBN-13: 978-1533224736
ISBN-10: 1533224730

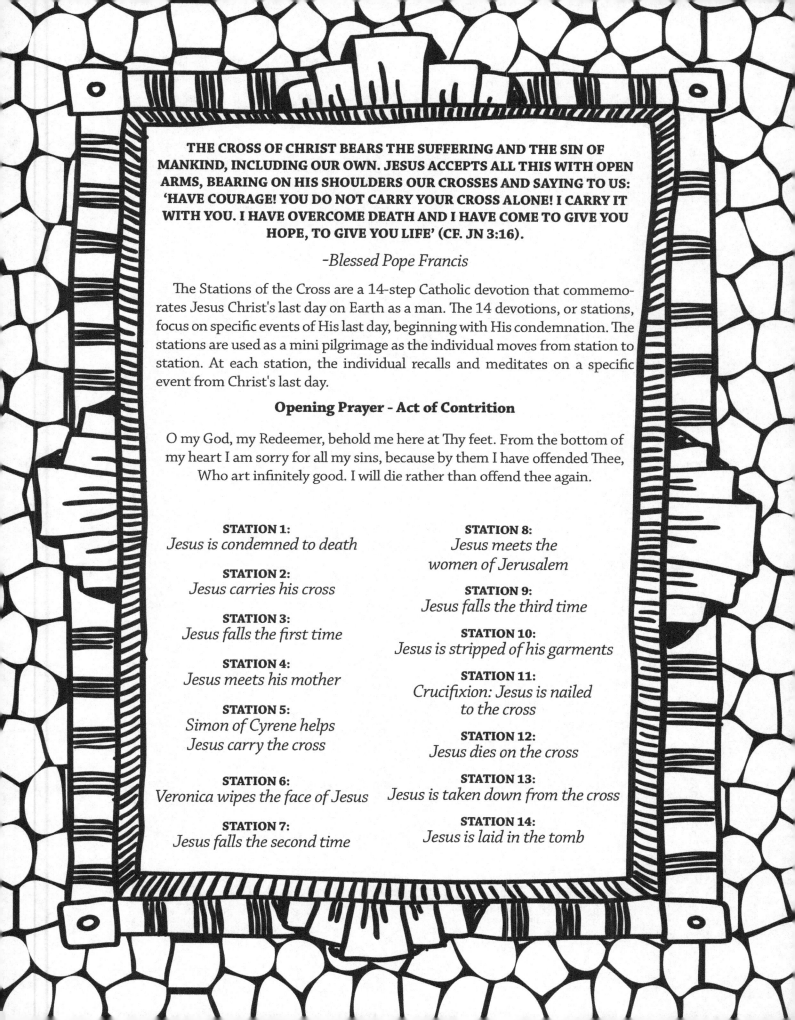

THE CROSS OF CHRIST BEARS THE SUFFERING AND THE SIN OF MANKIND, INCLUDING OUR OWN. JESUS ACCEPTS ALL THIS WITH OPEN ARMS, BEARING ON HIS SHOULDERS OUR CROSSES AND SAYING TO US: 'HAVE COURAGE! YOU DO NOT CARRY YOUR CROSS ALONE! I CARRY IT WITH YOU. I HAVE OVERCOME DEATH AND I HAVE COME TO GIVE YOU HOPE, TO GIVE YOU LIFE' (CF. JN 3:16).

-Blessed Pope Francis

The Stations of the Cross are a 14-step Catholic devotion that commemorates Jesus Christ's last day on Earth as a man. The 14 devotions, or stations, focus on specific events of His last day, beginning with His condemnation. The stations are used as a mini pilgrimage as the individual moves from station to station. At each station, the individual recalls and meditates on a specific event from Christ's last day.

Opening Prayer - Act of Contrition

O my God, my Redeemer, behold me here at Thy feet. From the bottom of my heart I am sorry for all my sins, because by them I have offended Thee, Who art infinitely good. I will die rather than offend thee again.

STATION 1:
Jesus is condemned to death

STATION 2:
Jesus carries his cross

STATION 3:
Jesus falls the first time

STATION 4:
Jesus meets his mother

STATION 5:
Simon of Cyrene helps Jesus carry the cross

STATION 6:
Veronica wipes the face of Jesus

STATION 7:
Jesus falls the second time

STATION 8:
Jesus meets the women of Jerusalem

STATION 9:
Jesus falls the third time

STATION 10:
Jesus is stripped of his garments

STATION 11:
Crucifixion: Jesus is nailed to the cross

STATION 12:
Jesus dies on the cross

STATION 13:
Jesus is taken down from the cross

STATION 14:
Jesus is laid in the tomb

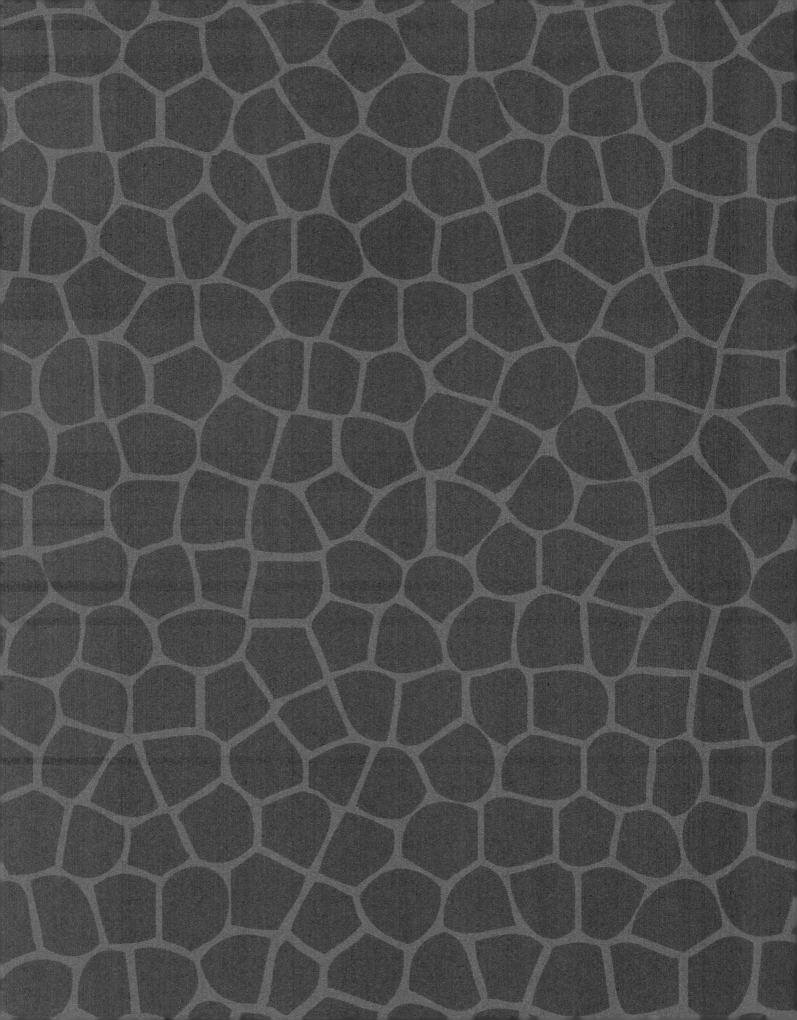

STATION I

PILATE *Condemns* JESUS TO DIE

SO JESUS CAME OUT, WEARING THE CROWN OF THORNS AND THE PURPLE CLOAK. AND HE SAID TO THEM,

"BEHOLD, THE MAN!"

JOHN 19:5

"*We adore you, O Christ and we bless you. Because by your holy cross you have redeemed the world.*"

LORD JESUS, YOU ARE THE KINGS OF KINGS AND THE LORD OF LORDS, YOU HAVE BEEN HUMILIATED BECAUSE OF MY PRIDE, I AM SORRY TO HAVE ENTHRONED THE KINGDOM OF THE WORLD IN MY HEART, PLEASE GRANT ME TO ATTACH MYSELF ONLY TO YOU.

STATION I

STATION I

STATION I
PRAYERS & DEVOTIONS

STATION II

JESUS *Accepts* HIS CROSS

RATHER, HE EMPTIED HIMSELF, TAKING THE FORM OF A SLAVE, COMING IN HUMAN LIKENESS; AND FOUND HUMAN IN APPEARANCE.

PHILIPPIANS 2:7

"WE ADORE YOU, O CHRIST AND WE BLESS YOU. BECAUSE BY YOUR HOLY CROSS YOU HAVE REDEEMED THE WORLD."

JESUS, YOU CARRIED THAT HEAVY CROSS UPON YOUR WOUNDED SHOULDER, AND YET THE WEIGHT OF THE CROSS WAS MY SINFULNESS, SO I REPENT OF MY SINS AND I BEG YOU TO GRANT ME YOUR SALVATION. FORGIVE ME LORD THAT I HAVE FAILED TO DO YOUR HOLY WILL.

STATION II

STATION II

STATION II
PRAYERS & DEVOTIONS

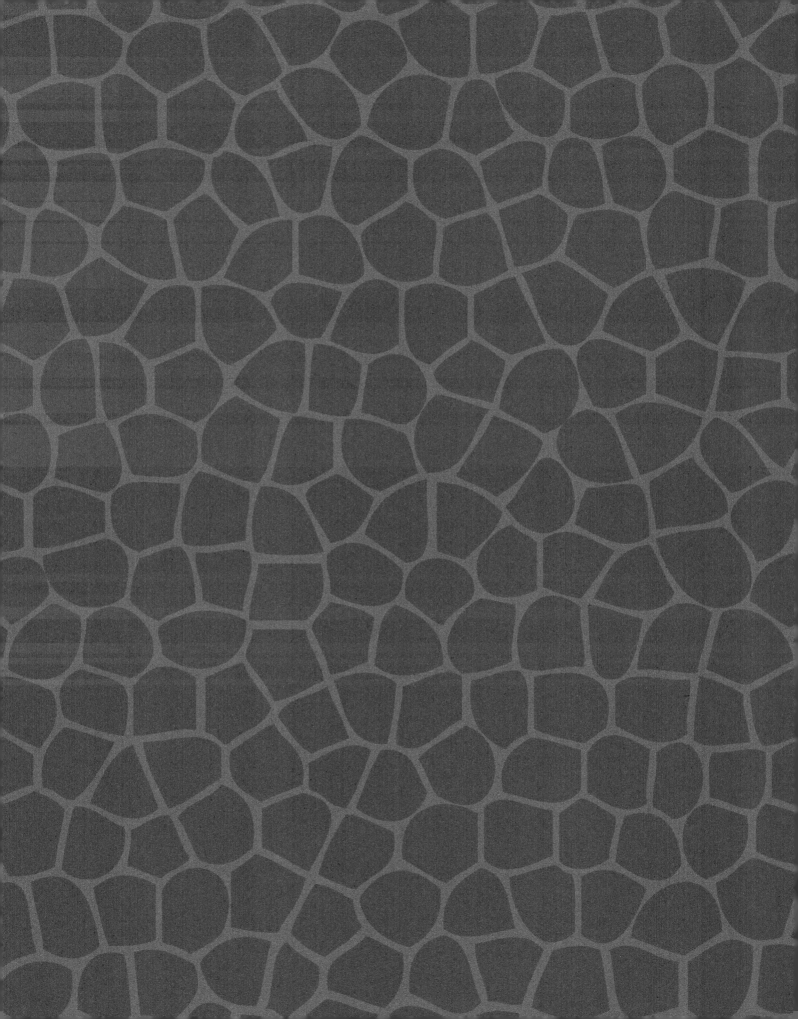

STATION III

JESUS *Falls the* FIRST TIME

HERE IS MY SERVANT WHOM I UPHOLD, MY CHOSEN ONE WITH WHOM I AM PLEASED. UPON HIM I HAVE PUT MY SPIRIT; HE SHALL BRING FORTH JUSTICE TO THE NATIONS. HE WILL NOT CRY OUT, NOR SHOUT, NOR MAKE HIS VOICE HEARD IN THE STREET.

ISAIAH 42:1-2

"WE ADORE YOU, O CHRIST AND WE BLESS YOU. BECAUSE BY YOUR HOLY CROSS YOU HAVE REDEEMED THE WORLD."

LORD IN THIS FIRST FALL YOU ATONED FOR THE ORIGINAL SIN OF ALL HUMANITY, I THANK YOU AND PRAISE FOR YOUR UNLIMITED LOVE FOR ME, PLEASE LORD, HELP ME NOT TO SIN ANY MORE.

STATION III

STATION III

STATION III
PRAYERS & DEVOTIONS

STATION IV

JESUS *Meets His* AFFLICTED MOTHER

COME, ALL WHO PASS BY THE WAY, PAY ATTENTION AND SEE: IS THERE ANY PAIN LIKE MY PAIN, WHICH HAS BEEN RUTHLESSLY INFLICTED UPON ME, WITH WHICH THE LORD HAS TORMENTED ME ON THE DAY OF HIS BLAZING WRATH?

LAMENTATIONS 1:12

"WE ADORE YOU, O CHRIST AND WE BLESS YOU. BECAUSE BY YOUR HOLY CROSS YOU HAVE REDEEMED THE WORLD."

SORROWFUL MOTHER MARY, ALLOW ME TO SHARE YOUR SORROW SO THAT THE HOLY PASSION OF MY LORD REMAINS ALWAYS VIVID WITHIN ME AS A RE-MINDER OF GOD'S LOVE FOR ME. COME TO MEET ME ALSO IN MY SORROWFUL JOURNEY TO THE LORD.

STATION IV

STATION IV

STATION IV
PRAYERS & DEVOTIONS

STATION V

SIMON *Helps Jesus* CARRY THE CROSS

THEY PRESSED INTO SERVICE A PASSER-BY, SIMON, A CYRENIAN, WHO WAS COMING IN FROM THE COUNTRY, THE FATHER OF ALEXANDER AND RUFUS, TO CARRY HIS CROSS.

MARK 15:21

"WE ADORE YOU, O CHRIST AND WE BLESS YOU. BECAUSE BY YOUR HOLY CROSS YOU HAVE REDEEMED THE WORLD."

LORD YOU WANT US TO SHARE THE CROSS WITH YOU BY SHARING AND ALLEVIATING THE SUFFERINGS OF THOSE IN NEED, GRANT ME TO HAVE A HEART FULL OF CHARITY AND LOVE FOR MY NEIGHBOR.

STATION V

STATION V

STATION V
PRAYERS & DEVOTIONS

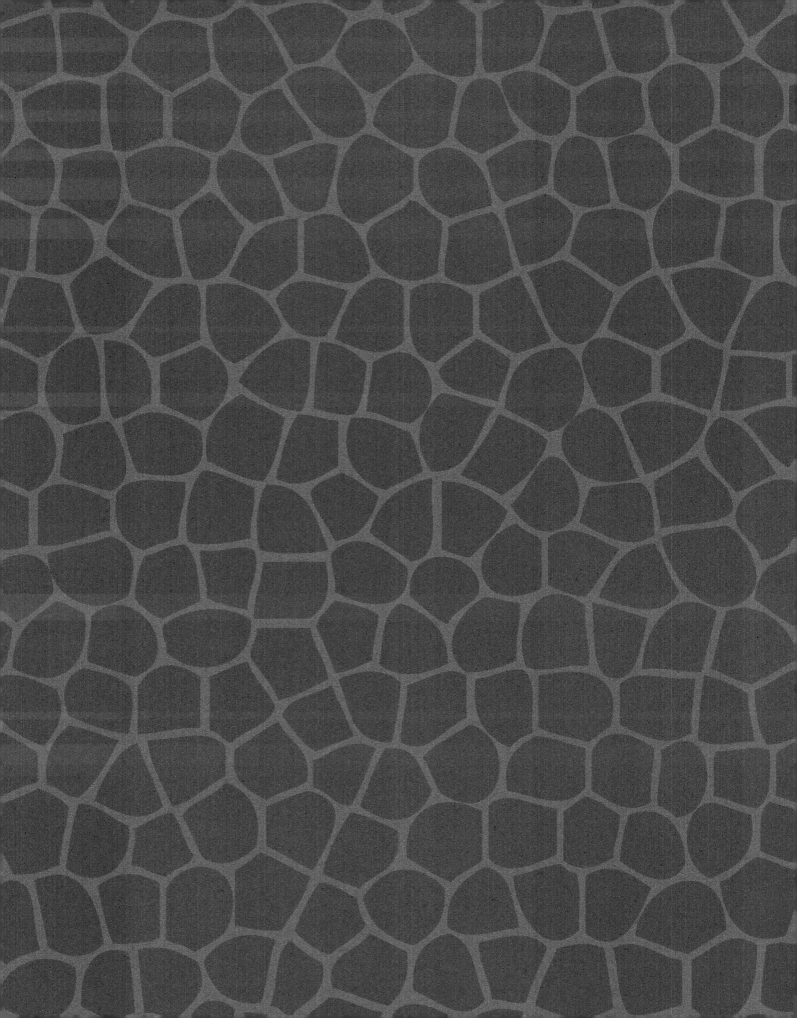

STATION VI

VERONICA *Offers Her* VEIL TO JESUS

HE WAS SPURNED AND AVOIDED BY MEN, A MAN OF SUFFERING, KNOWING PAIN, LIKE ONE FROM WHOM YOU TURN YOUR FACE, SPURNED, AND WE HELD HIM IN NO ESTEEM. YET IT WAS OUR PAIN THAT HE BORE, OUR SUFFERINGS HE ENDURED. WE THOUGHT OF HIM AS STRICKEN, STRUCK DOWN BY GOD AND AFFLICTED.

MARK 15:21

"WE ADORE YOU, O CHRIST AND WE BLESS YOU. BECAUSE BY YOUR HOLY CROSS YOU HAVE REDEEMED THE WORLD."

LORD, YOU HAVE CREATED US FOR YOUR GLORY, PLEASE HELP US BY WIPING THE STAINS OF OUR SOULS WITH YOUR PRECIOUS BLOOD TO RESTORE YOUR IMAGE IN US.

STATION VI

STATION VI

STATION VI
PRAYERS & DEVOTIONS

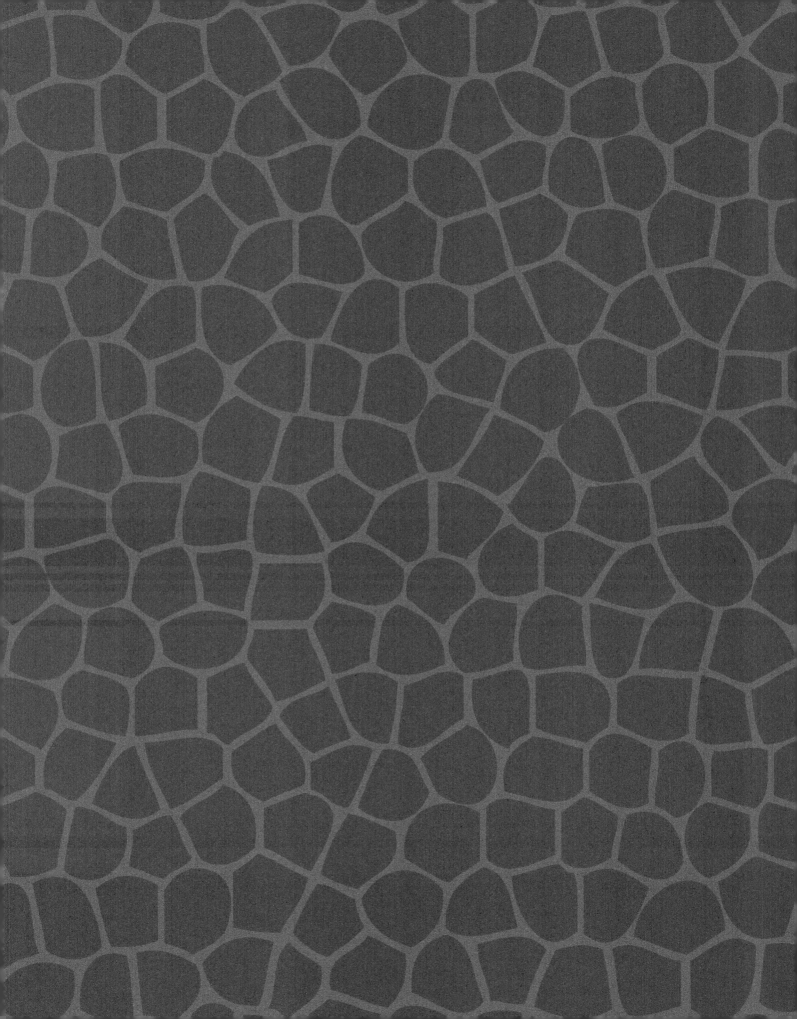

STATION VII

JESUS FALLS
The Second TIME

YET IT WAS OUR PAIN THAT HE BORE, OUR SUFFERINGS HE ENDURED. WE THOUGHT OF HIM AS STRICKEN, STRUCK DOWN BY GOD AND AFFLICTED, BUT HE WAS PIERCED FOR OUR SINS, CRUSHED FOR OUR INIQUITY. HE BORE THE PUNISHMENT THAT MAKES US WHOLE, BY HIS WOUNDS WE WERE HEALED.

ISAIAH 53:4-5

"WE ADORE YOU, O CHRIST AND WE BLESS YOU. BECAUSE BY YOUR HOLY CROSS YOU HAVE REDEEMED THE WORLD."

BY THIS SECOND FALL YOU CONFIRM HOW WEAK WE ARE, HELP US LORD TO OVERCOME OUR WEAKNESSES WITH THE STRENGTH OF YOUR SUFFERINGS. TEACH US HOW TO LOVE GOOD AND TO HATE EVIL.

STATION VII

STATION VII

STATION VII
PRAYERS & DEVOTIONS

STATION VIII

JESUS *Speaks to* THE WOMEN

A LARGE CROWD OF PEOPLE FOLLOWED JESUS, INCLUDING MANY WOMEN WHO MOURNED AND LAMENTED HIM. JESUS TURNED TO THEM AND SAID, "DAUGHTERS OF JERUSALEM, DO NOT WEEP FOR ME; WEEP INSTEAD FOR YOURSELVES AND FOR YOUR CHILDREN.

LUKE 23:27-28

"WE ADORE YOU, O CHRIST AND WE BLESS YOU. BECAUSE BY YOUR HOLY CROSS YOU HAVE REDEEMED THE WORLD."

LORD, IN OUR HUMAN WEAKNESS WE ARE SO CONCERNED TO LIVE OUR LIVES WITHOUT DISCOMFORT AND PAIN, AND YET YOU TELL US THAT IT IS MORE IMPORTANT TO SEEK THE KINGDOM OF HEAVEN AND TO WEEP FOR OUR SINS IN ORDER TO GAIN ETERNAL LIFE.

STATION VIII

STATION VIII

STATION VIII
PRAYERS & DEVOTIONS

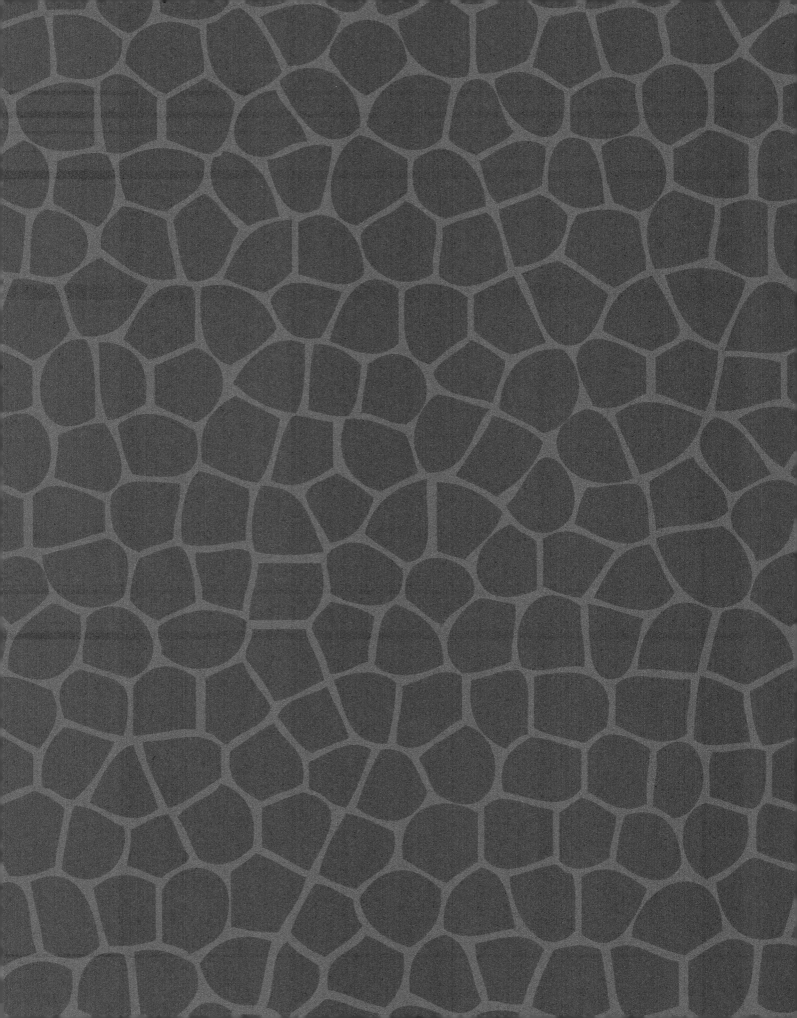

STATION IX

JESUS *Falls the* THIRD TIME

WE HAD ALL GONE ASTRAY LIKE SHEEP, ALL FOLLOWING OUR OWN WAY; BUT THE LORD LAID UPON HIM THE GUILT OF US ALL. THOUGH HARSHLY TREATED, HE SUBMITTED AND DID NOT OPEN HIS MOUTH; LIKE A LAMB LED TO SLAUGHTER OR A SHEEP SILENT BEFORE SHEARERS, HE DID NOT OPEN HIS MOUTH.

ISAIAH 53:6-7

"*WE ADORE YOU, O CHRIST AND WE BLESS YOU. BECAUSE BY YOUR HOLY CROSS YOU HAVE REDEEMED THE WORLD.*"

LORD YOU HAVE STRETCHED YOUR GENEROSITY TO THE LIMITS, PLEASE FORGIVE US FOR THE MANY TIMES THAT WE SIN AND DON'T REMEMBER WHAT PAIN YOU HAD TO GO THROUGH TO REDEEM US.

STATION IX

STATION IX

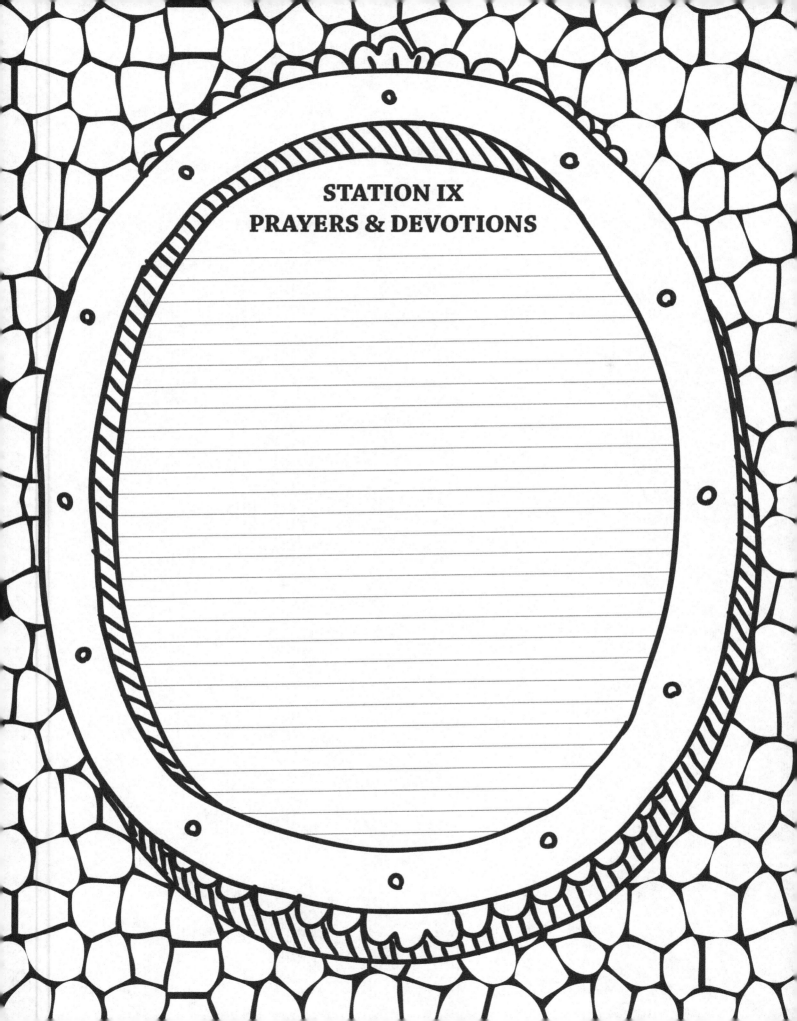

STATION IX
PRAYERS & DEVOTIONS

STATION X

JESUS IS *Stripped of* HIS GARMENTS

WHEN THE SOLDIERS HAD CRUCIFIED JESUS, THEY TOOK HIS CLOTHES AND DIVIDED THEM INTO FOUR SHARES, A SHARE FOR EACH SOLDIER. THEY ALSO TOOK HIS TUNIC, BUT THE TUNIC WAS SEAMLESS, WOVEN IN ONE PIECE FROM THE TOP DOWN.

JOHN 19:23

I CAN COUNT ALL MY BONES. THEY STARE AT ME AND GLOAT.

PSALM 22:18

"WE ADORE YOU, O CHRIST AND WE BLESS YOU. BECAUSE BY YOUR HOLY CROSS YOU HAVE REDEEMED THE WORLD."

LORD WHAT THEY DID TO YOU IS WHAT WE DO TO OUR SOULS, WE STRIP YOUR IMAGE WHICH IS GIVEN TO US IN BAPTISM AND WE CORRUPT THE TEMPLES OF YOUR GLORY. CLOTHE OUR SOULS ONCE MORE WITH THE ROBES OF YOUR DIVINE MERCY

STATION X

STATION X

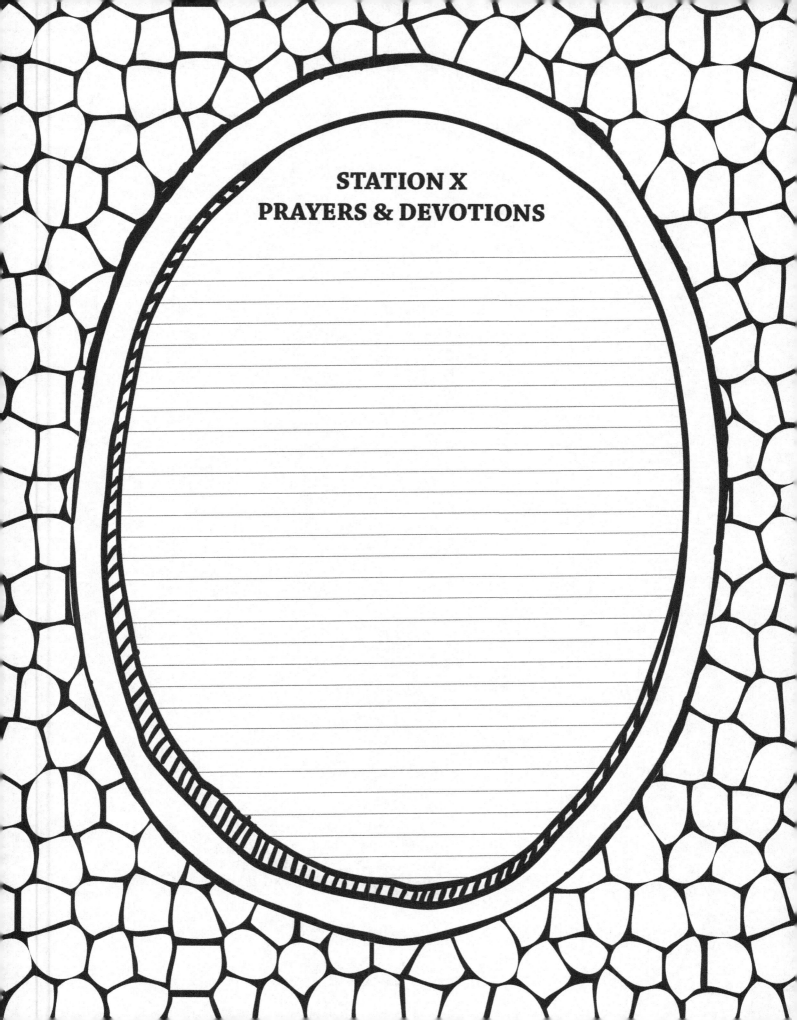

STATION X
PRAYERS & DEVOTIONS

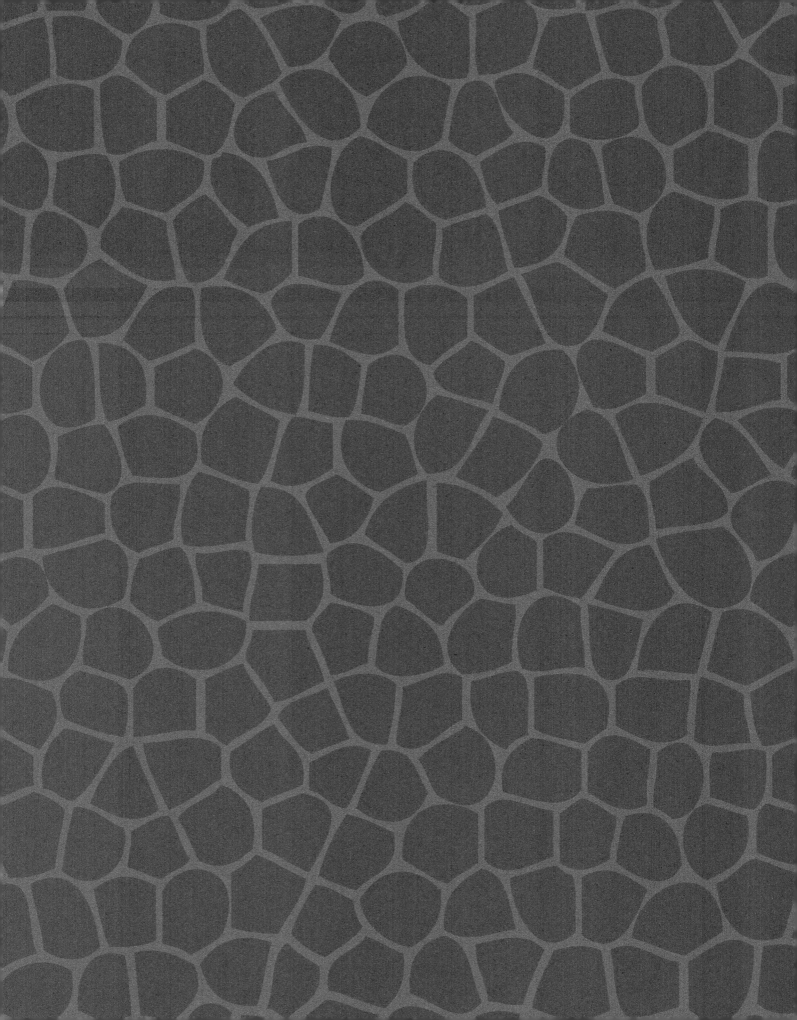

STATION XI

JESUS IS *Nailed to* THE CROSS

AND JUST AS MOSES LIFTED UP THE SERPENT IN THE DESERT, SO MUST THE SON OF MAN BE LIFTED UP, SO THAT EVERYONE WHO BELIEVES IN HIM MAY HAVE ETERNAL LIFE.

JOHN 19:23

"WE ADORE YOU, O CHRIST AND WE BLESS YOU. BECAUSE BY YOUR HOLY CROSS YOU HAVE REDEEMED THE WORLD."

LORD, YOU HAVE CALLED ME TO BE YOUR DISCIPLE, TO DENY MYSELF AND TO FOLLOW YOU. AS I COME BEFORE YOU, I CRUCIFY MY WILL TO YOURS, I CRUCIFY ALL THE TEMPTATIONS OF THE WORLD, THE DEVIL AND THE FLESH AND I PRAY FOR TOTAL SUBMISSION TO YOUR HOLY WILL.

STATION XI

STATION XI

STATION XI
PRAYERS & DEVOTIONS

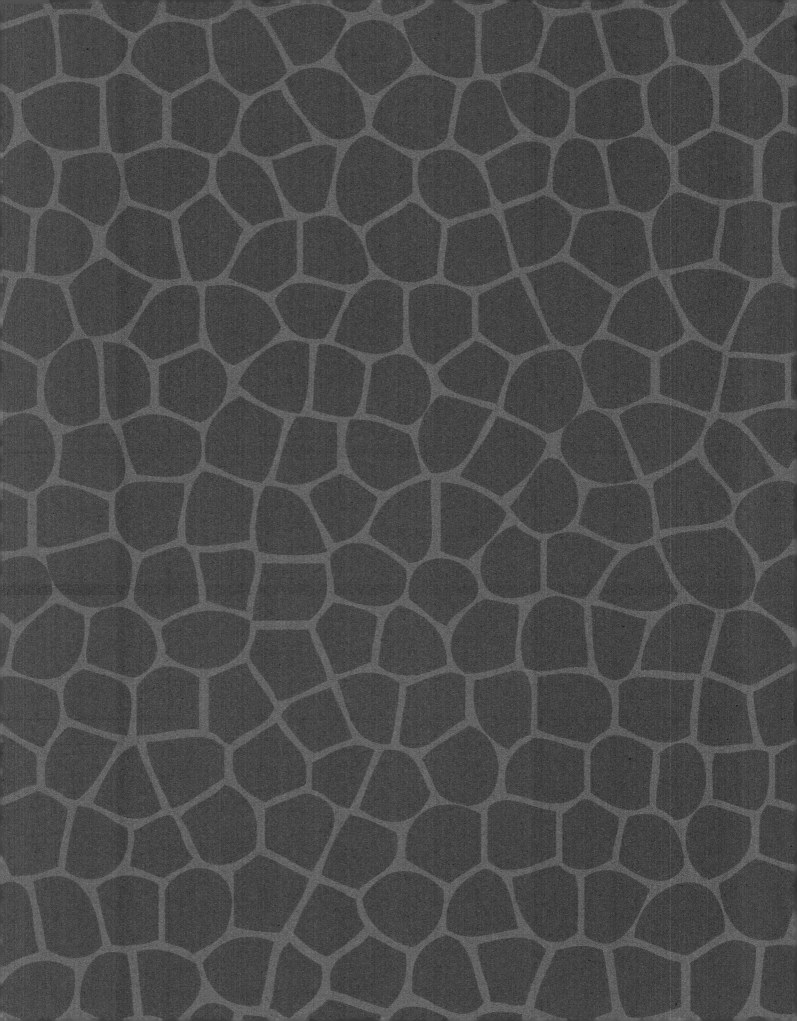

STATION XII

JESUS *Dies Upon* THE CROSS

JESUS ANSWERED HIM, "FRIEND, DO WHAT YOU HAVE COME FOR." THEN STEPPING FORWARD THEY LAID HANDS ON JESUS AND ARRESTED HIM.

MATTHEW 26:50

"WE ADORE YOU, O CHRIST AND WE BLESS YOU. BECAUSE BY YOUR HOLY CROSS YOU HAVE REDEEMED THE WORLD."

LORD, IT IS HERE ON THE CROSS THAT YOU ASK THE FATHER TO FORGIVE ME, HERE YOU GIVE ME YOUR MOTHER TO BE MY HEAVENLY MOTHER, HERE YOU PROMISE ME TO BE WITH YOU IN YOUR KINGDOM. I COME TO MEET YOU AND TO PARTAKE OF YOUR HOLY SACRIFICES AS I RECEIVE YOU IN HOLY COMMUNION.

STATION XII

STATION XII

STATION XII
PRAYERS & DEVOTIONS

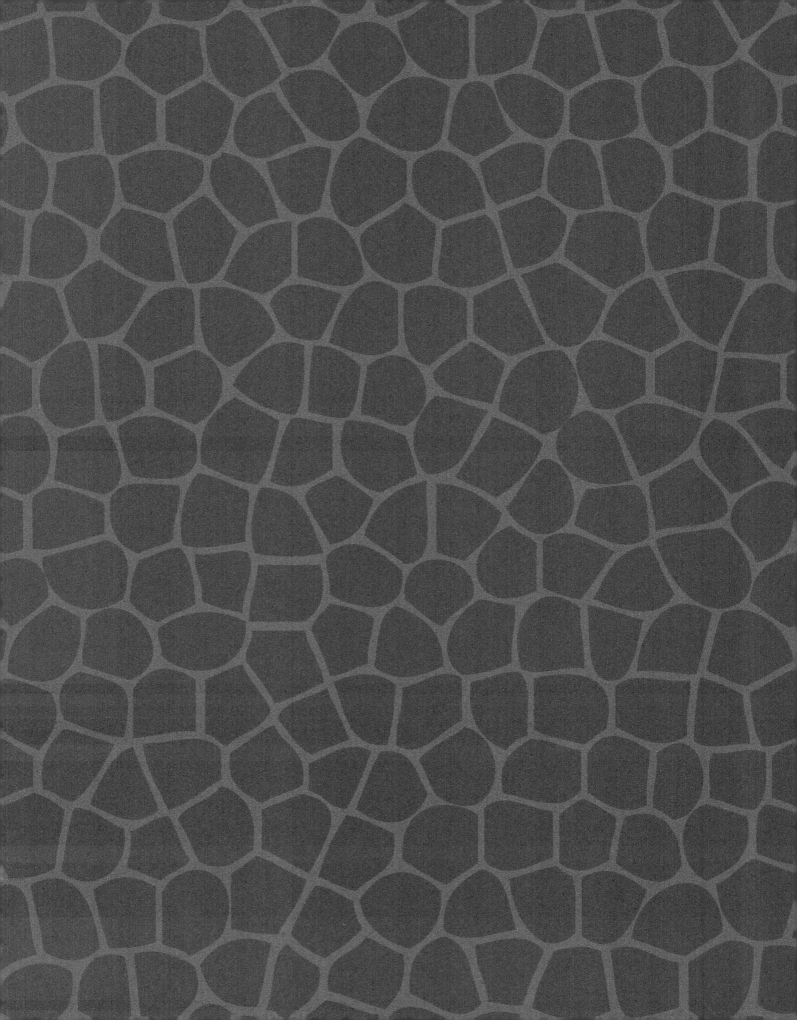

STATION XIII

JESUS IS *Taken Down* FROM THE CROSS

I WILL POUR OUT ON THE HOUSE OF DAVID AND ON THE INHABITANTS OF JERUSALEM A SPIRIT OF MERCY AND SUPPLICATION, SO THAT WHEN THEY LOOK ON HIM WHOM THEY HAVE THRUST THROUGH, THEY WILL MOURN FOR HIM AS ONE MOURNS FOR AN ONLY CHILD, AND THEY WILL GRIEVE FOR HIM AS ONE GRIEVES OVER A FIRSTBORN.

ZECHARIAH 12:10

"*We adore you, O Christ and we bless you. Because by your holy cross you have redeemed the world.*"

"LORD, AS YOU RESTED IN THE ARMS OF YOUR MOTHER, SO I WANT TO REST IN YOUR SACRED HEART, RECEIVE MY BROKENNESS AND HEAL ME FOR EVERLASTING LIFE."

STATION XIII

STATION XIII

STATION XIII
PRAYERS & DEVOTIONS

STATION XIV

JESUS IS *Placed in the* SEPULCHER

HAVING BOUGHT A LINEN CLOTH, HE TOOK HIM DOWN, WRAPPED HIM IN THE LINEN CLOTH AND LAID HIM IN A TOMB THAT HAD BEEN HEWN OUT OF THE ROCK. THEN HE ROLLED A STONE AGAINST THE ENTRANCE TO THE TOMB.

MARK 15:46

"*We adore you, o christ and we bless you. Because by your holy cross you have redeemed the world.*"

LORD LET ME DIE IN YOU AND REMAIN BURIED WITHIN ME, I LOOK FORWARD TO THE MOMENT OF THE RESURRECTION FROM THE DEAD WHEN YOU WILL REVEAL YOUR GLORY TO ME. FOR NOW LET ME ADORE YOU IN THE BLESSED SACRAMENT AND GRANT THE GRACE TO LIVE A HOLY LIFE.

STATION XIV

STATION XIV

STATION XIV
PRAYERS & DEVOTIONS

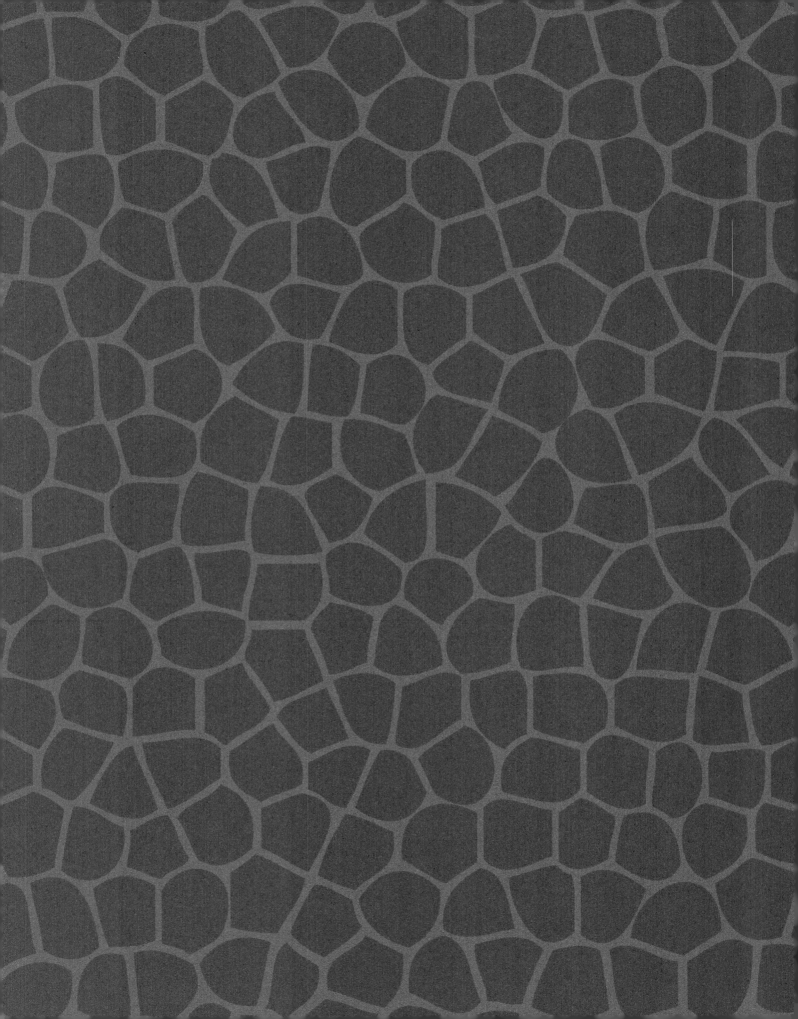

BE SURE TO FOLLOW US
ON SOCIAL MEDIA FOR THE
LATEST NEWS, SNEAK
PEEKS, & GIVEAWAYS

@drawntofaith

Drawn To Faith

@drawntofaith

ADD YOURSELF TO OUR MONTHLY
NEWSLETTER FOR FREE DIGITAL
DOWNLOADS AND DISCOUNT CODES

www.drawntofaith.com/newsletter

CHECK OUT OUR OTHER BOOKS!

www.drawntofaith.com

   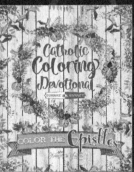